REA[...] YOU[...] BE YOUTUBE FAMOUS.

WILL EAGLE

Published in 2020 by
Laurence King Publishing Ltd
361–373 City Road
London EC1V 1LR
e-mail: enquiries@laurenceking.com
www.laurenceking.com

This book was designed and produced by
Laurence King Publishing Ltd, London.

Read This If You Want To Be YouTube Famous
is based on an original concept by Henry Carroll.

A catalogue record for this book
is available from the British Library.
ISBN: 978 1 78627 513 4

Senior editor: Andrew Roff
Designer: Alexandre Coco
Picture research: Sandra Assersohn
Production: Davina Cheung

All images are credited to the YouTuber on the page,
except for those on page 111, which are credited to
Obsev Studios (top) and Steve Earle (bottom).

Printed in China

Laurence King Publishing is committed
to ethical and sustainable production. We are
proud participants in The Book Chain Project®
bookchainproject.com

This book is not authorized by or associated
with YouTube or any other company.

Please note follower numbers and other statistics
were correct as of the original date of publication
but are subject to change.

For Nanci, Ringle, Franteen and Mamasweeta.
With a special dedication to Grant Thompson, who believed in random acts of kindness.

READ THIS IF YOU WANT TO BE YOUTUBE FAMOUS.

WILL EAGLE

contents

Who doesn't want to be YouTube famous?

The promise of millions of fans and money rolling in every month from a career that allows you to make videos that express your creativity is enormously appealing, and it seems that all you need to get started is your smartphone. But how do you grow from a single video with no views, when hundreds of hours of video content are being uploaded to YouTube every minute? How do you stand out?

The secrets are in this book, where 45 of the world's top YouTubers (along with some of the weirdest ones) have shared their wisdom to set you up for success before you even hit record. They will explain everything from how to find your passion to making videos for a popular niche, and from handling trolls to making money. These YouTubers all share a creative spirit and the tenacity not to give up.

If you've ever wanted to be a YouTuber, this book will help you get started. If you're already making videos, it'll help you kick things into gear so you can finally live the dream of getting mobbed by fans at VidCon.

Let's do this.

/ denotes either a shortened URL
or a term that you can search to
find the channel easily

Don't overthink it

Pick up your phone and start recording your first video without thinking too much about it. When I started, mobile phones weren't as sophisticated as they are now, but today you can get ones that record HD and 4K video, so just start. It doesn't have to be perfect, just record it, whether it's handheld or with your phone leaning against a stack of books. Talk about whatever you want to talk about. You can use apps like iMovie to do some simple editing, and that's all it takes to get your first video made.

Matt's story

I was working as an accountant and, despite doing well, got laid off. When that happened, I realized that there's a lot of risk involved in working for someone else; despite being smart and good at your job, you can get laid off any time. YouTube let me be my own boss, taking back some of that control. I experimented with different videos, starting with comedy skits, and over time I learned what worked and what didn't. I went heavier on the list format after I saw that it popped, and since then I've continued making list videos.

/MATTHEWSANTORO
Matt Santoro
Subscribers: > 6.3m

Favourite YouTubers:
/WatchMojo
/PewDiePie
/markiplierGAME

Aboot

/MRMCCRUDDENMICHAEL

Michael McCrudden
Subscribers: > 3m

Favourite YouTubers:
/sxePhil (Philip DeFranco)
/LoganPaulVlogs
/MatthewSantoro

Pick what you love

Look, if this works out for you and you become a successful YouTuber, you're gonna do it every day for a long time, so if you don't love it, don't do it. If what you make videos about isn't true to who you are and what you love, you're gonna get sick of it quickly. Look inwards at what you've been passionate about your entire life, what separates you from everyone else on this planet, and use that to foster the thesis of your channel.

Michael's story

For me, it all magically came together over a ten-year journey. All I'd wanted to be was an MTV VJ, so I went to college for TV, learned about film, how to write and how to record. I took on TV projects to learn different skills to help me get set up for a career in TV, but when being a VJ didn't happen, I found YouTube. I was working with no budget, which was completely different from TV. I started small, and experimented; I'd written a movie about Jim Carrey, my idol, and I decided to make a video about before he was famous. It got tons of views, and really set things off for me.

Find a niche

You don't need millions of subscribers if you want to make a living from YouTube. There are already tons of people making lists, doing makeup tutorials and unboxing videos, so think about why someone would want to watch your channel. If your point of view is what makes you different, but will appeal to a few thousand people, not a few million, that's OK – do that. The great thing about YouTube is that you can make videos about random things like marble racing and find tremendous success. There are unlimited channels, and it keeps growing, so find a smaller niche and appeal to that.

Sam's story

I started in music journalism, and back in 2007, in an attempt to avoid anything like a 9–5 desk job, I pitched the editor to let me make videos for our YouTube channel, interviewing bands. I parlayed that into jobs like being a host on MTV News, but found myself longing for the freedom I'd had before. I'd been working for a medium-sized media company, and part of that was a YouTube channel. When they wanted to shut it down, they let me buy it from them, and I've run it since then, making videos about ninja turtle metal and jihadist rap.

/THISEXISTS
Sam Sutherland
Subscribers: > 365k

Favourite YouTubers:
/NerdyAndQuirky
(Sabrina Cruz)
/ContraPoints
/Robs70986987
(Rob Scallon)

Finding your niche

Sam from This Exists (see p.12) says to find your niche, a space that has a large viewership but that you alone can own. But how do you find a niche? Here's a handy-dandy checklist.

Go for a deep dive

Start by spending a few hours just watching videos on YouTube. Search for a video related to what you think you'd like to make, and just hang out watching all the related and 'up next' videos. Who knows where you'll end up, but you'll uncover interesting angles for your topic that you might not have considered before, and that might inspire your own unique take.

Make autofill your friend

When you type something in the YouTube search bar, it'll autofill with popular searches. This is gold, because it tells you what people might be looking for. Try it now. Type in anything. I tried 'Dog costume', which is pretty generic, and got autofills for … carrying pumpkin, for Halloween, with arms, DIY, for humans, carrying beer and more. Each of these is a potential niche you could make videos about. Explore them.

Make sure it's a popular niche

So you've decided to focus exclusively on DIY pumpkin dog costumes. I fully support that. To be sure there's enough interest in this niche, answer these questions:

Do the videos that exist have lots of views, and are the videos recent?

Do these channels have subscribers, and are people commenting?

Do you think all the pumpkin-dog-costume videos have been made already, or can you bring something new?

The final check

Ask yourself the crucial question:

'Will I always be passionate about making only pumpkin-dog-costume videos?'

Set up your YouTube channel.

DO
everything
WITH
love

hello HELLO HELLO
hello HELLO hello
HELLO hello HELLO
HI hi Hi!
hello hello
HELLO HI
HI hi HELLO
hello
HELLO HI hello
hello HELLO
HELLO hello
HI hello hi HI
hi HELLO HI hi
HELLO hello HELLO
HI HI hello hello
hello HI
HELLO
HELLO HELLO
greetings hello

/AMANDARACHLEE
Amanda Rach Lee
Subscribers: > 1.4m

Favourite YouTubers:
/sxePhil (Philip DeFranco)
/JunsKitchen
/JennaMarbles

Consistency is key

Be consistent with your posting. Lots of people starting out get impatient. I know it can be discouraging at first because you might not get as many views as you expect, but consistently posting videos about topics that you enjoy will help you grow in an authentic way. I was persistent with my channel and only really started to see proper growth after three or four years. Within those years, there was no promise of success or guarantee of YouTube becoming my full-time career, but I kept doing it simply because I enjoyed creating and interacting with my audience. I feel like many YouTubers don't have huge success at the beginning. I found that the growth was a slow build at the beginning, but it became exponential over time, so stick with it and stay consistent!

Amanda's story

I was an avid viewer of YouTube for years before I started. I got a camera for my 15th birthday, so I filmed something and posted it. It was fun, so I kept going, but I actually kept it a secret for a year before telling my friends and family about it. I started out making fashion and beauty videos, but after about two years and maybe 100,000 subscribers, I switched to making videos about my true passions: art, journalling and doodling. I was able to build an even bigger audience of people who liked my style of accessible art.

Make it sustainable

Making videos is like going on a diet. If you want to lose weight, an extreme diet won't be sustainable for much more than a month. If you spend a lot of time making videos but can't sustain that effort, you probably have the wrong idea. We use the hydraulic press in our family's metal workshop to crush things. It's a sustainable, easily repeatable format that has been popular. I started working 90 hours a week, but now it's more manageable, about 50 hours. You need to make videos that you can keep creating and publishing over time.

Hydraulic Press Channel's story

I'd seen similar videos on YouTube, like putting hot metal objects on surfaces to see what happened. There's a lot of interesting stuff in our workshop, and the hydraulic press is only used about once a month, so I looked on YouTube to see if there were other videos using a press to crush objects and there weren't! I made the channel and created the first ten videos, and the format is still much the same. When someone posted one of our videos on Reddit we got 2m views in one day, and within two months we had 1m subscribers. My family are proud. It feels normal now to do this.

/HYDRAULICPRESSCHANNEL
/BEYONDTHEPRESS
Hydraulic Press Channel
Subscribers: > 2.3m
> 565k

Favourite YouTubers:
/JoergSprave
/IsaacArthur
/ScottManley

The power of vulnerability

/SHALOMBLAC
Shalom Blac
Subscribers: > 1.3m

Favourite YouTubers:
/TaliaJoy18
/LilPumpkinPie05
(Jackie Aina)
/JamersonJamessss
(James Butler)

Being vulnerable helped me get over many of my fears. I've adapted to being frank, and making videos where I open up about things that people might not talk about for fear of being judged. This has helped me grow my channel, and my self-esteem. I feel that even if just one person relates, I'm not alone, and I'm helping. I never thought I'd be where I am today because of how I looked, but by being vulnerable I took a potential disadvantage and made it a strength, which has helped me reach a bigger audience.

Shalom's story

I came across a YouTuber named Talia who was making videos about makeup and unboxing things even though she was battling cancer and had gone bald from her treatment. I was bald too, and I didn't realize someone could be so courageous and put themselves out there. I'm a burns survivor and I came to YouTube to learn how to conceal my scars, but it was difficult because few people have scars like mine. I had to teach myself. I'd been bullied at school and online, but still I started my channel showing other burns survivors what I'd learned. Lots of people asked about my story, so I made a video explaining what happened, and things took off from there.

Don't post your first 15 videos

Seriously. You'll thank me later. You think you change, but it's really just that you become yourself. When you sit down in front of your camera for the first time, it's awkward. The real you will come out later, when you're more comfortable, so film a ton of videos, start creating your style and feeling more comfortable without posting them. When you finally post, the videos will be more you than those you initially made. Every creator I've said this to said they wished they had done it, so don't post your first 15 videos. For real.

/MOLLYBURKEOFFICIAL
Molly Burke
Subscribers: > 1.8m

Favourite YouTubers:
/Shane (Shane Dawson)
/SafiyaNygaard
/CaseyNeistat

Molly's story

In 2008 I lost my vision and experienced a phase of depression. I started watching YouTube, thinking it was just cat videos, but I found my community in the lifestyle and beauty vloggers. I'd binge-watch girls on YouTube who came to feel like my friends. I couldn't look in a shop window or read a magazine, but on YouTube I could listen to people talk about fashion and makeup, and I started trying things out. I figured things out that I couldn't see any more, which rebuilt my confidence. My audience says they love my makeup or my clothes – and I credit YouTube with making fashion and beauty advice from a blind girl possible.

Make yourself at home

It might seem obvious, but an important first step is getting your YouTube channel fully set up. It's your home on the platform, and giving it some love and attention right out of the gate is a great idea. Let's break down the anatomy of a channel, taking The Icing Artist (see p.30) as our example.

What's in a name?

Make the name of your YouTube channel something that represents you and what the channel is all about. You don't have to use your real name, so get creative.

Make it artful

You've got a large banner area to upload your own artwork. Some YouTubers use this space to communicate which videos they are posting on certain days.

Tease with a trailer

You can make a trailer video that plays for people who visit your channel but who haven't yet subscribed. Keep it short, sweet, fun and light, and explain what you and your videos are all about. Whatever you do, don't start with 'Welcome to my channel.' It's kinda lame.

Laurie Shannon "The Icing Artist" teaches the easy way to make WOW-worthy desserts with just a few simple tools and ingredients. Even the non-bakers will fall in love with the captivating and satisfying way Laurie makes her amazing creations. Constantly reinventing cakes and playing off (and poking fun at!) trends, there is always something new and exciting on The Icing Artist!

NEW yummy videos every week!

Have a cake question??? Shoot me an email!

Make a connection

You can add related channels to yours, such as other YouTube channels you might have, or the channels of your friends or favourite YouTubers. You can also add your various social profiles, such as Instagram and Facebook. You and your fans will be able to post text, images and links in your Community or Discussion tab.

Playing with playlists

When you start uploading your videos, make sure you add them to a playlist, and periodically check to see if you can create new playlists. Your videos (and other people's) can be combined many times into different playlists.

About

The About tab is where you post a description of who you are, what you're about, what people can expect and how they can get in touch with you. You can add an email for people to reach out to you. Just be clear how they should use it, for example if it's for business and partnerships enquiries only.

Get a dog

There's nothing like pets to bind us together, and Stella, my service dog, is a huge part of my channel and my life. She sits perfectly still while I talk about our lives; as my silent co-host, she's the perfect foil to anything I might say that is dicey or ridiculous. We make a twice-weekly Dog Vlog in which we talk about our daily life. I have a stutter, she has captions. We also have an animated cartoon series, 'Therapy Dog', every other Saturday. Stella's definitely a big reason for our appeal, and she brings her own demographic to the channel. I know some people tune in just for her.

Drew's story

Each new year I set goals. In 2014 I decided to do over 500 comedy shows (I did 592), and to create more content. I bought a camera and editing software, knowing nothing about either, and having set myself the goal of putting out two videos a week I started making YouTube films even though I hadn't decided on the format yet. I eventually landed on documenting my life, and came up with the idea for Dog Vlog. Now I'm posting more of my stand-up comedy, which is really why I created the channel in the first place, and I also post our animated show for those who want our content but in a different format.

/WORDSRHARD
Drew Lynch
Subscribers: > 2m

Favourite YouTubers:
/CaseyNeistat
/sxePhil (Philip DeFranco)
/HotBananaStud
(Brandon Rogers)

/UNSOLICITEDPROJECT
Adrianna and Sarah
Subscribers: > 430k

Favourite YouTubers:
/EveryFrameAPainting
/MirandaSings08
/BadLipReading

Laugh at yourself

We like to laugh at ourselves. We make videos that poke fun at LGBT issues; it lets us and our community take a break from being serious, have some fun and even consider things from a different angle. Try to find ways of laughing at yourself, along with your friends and your community. Of course, don't be mean-spirited. One of our first videos, 'Gay Women Will Marry your Boyfriends', which was a parody of a College Humor video, went viral and inspired us to make videos in which we have fun at our own expense.

Adrianna and Sarah's story

We both did internships in Los Angeles in film and TV production, and while we were there, Adrianna wrote a comedy pilot. We thought, 'Why don't we turn this into a web series?' We released four episodes on YouTube and were excited when we got about 800 views! We kept going, and some of our videos went viral, growing our subscribers from a handful to 200,000. We wanted to make longer-form scripted content, so we did a Kickstarter campaign to make our first feature film, which is now on Netflix. We've made another film since then, and have more projects in the pipeline.

Test test test

/THEICINGARTIST
Laurie Shannon
Subscribers: > 3.7m

Favourite YouTubers:
/llSuperwomanll
/CaseyNeistat
/RosannaPansino

I'm a strong believer in not assuming something's going to work, so we test everything. It took me a while to figure out my audience and how to connect with them on a personal level. I tested different styles of content and found that people love seeing their favourite characters, animals and foods turned into cake. Cake compilations also performed incredibly well – our most popular now has over 150m views. I'd test 10 or 15 thumbnails and found that the colour yellow and cakes with faces did better. I'd also test different titles, like 'How to Make a Bunny Cake' vs. 'The Cutest Bunny Cake that Hopped off the Table'. Testing is what helped me go from 80,000 subscribers to 2.5m in a year and a half. My advice is to always test everything.

Laurie's story

I was working as a cabinet maker but I wanted a more creative job, so I started working in a bakery. Although it was artistic, it was a minimum-wage job just pushing out cakes. My husband and I decided to try YouTube. Without knowing how to operate a camera or create content, I made my first video in my parents' basement. I knew I wanted to work from home and I thought if I worked hard enough maybe it could supplement my income. I worked every evening and weekend while working a full-time job for three years to make sure I never missed a video. Now my husband and I work on it full-time with our growing team.

Don't pigeonhole yourself

/SHANNONBOODRAM
Shan Boody
Subscribers: > 440k

Favourite YouTubers:
/SchoolofLifeChannel
/TEDtalksDirector
/GetTheGuyTeam
(Matthew Hussey)

Working with a big company always makes me appreciate my YouTube channel more, because there I have complete freedom to do what I want. I've always been a sex educator, so my fans know what they're gonna hear about, but they don't know how they're gonna hear it. It could be an interview, a show, a collaboration, a commentary, it could be scripted. I feel like a performer, and even though I stick to my topic, I don't pigeonhole myself when it comes to storytelling. People are excited when you provide something different, and if you don't restrict yourself creatively, you protect yourself from getting bored by your content.

Shan's story

I'd put out a book on sex education in 2009, and was running a blog with a friend at the time. Back then YouTube was just a place to upload and store our videos. We ended the blog in 2011, around the time being a YouTuber started to become a real career opportunity. I was stubborn about embracing YouTube at first, as I'd made a book, been in TV shows and been in three pilots that didn't get picked up, but I thought I'd give YouTube a try again. Now, I probably won't ever leave.

Before you hit record

You've done your hair, you're dressed cute AF, and you've even practised how you look and sound in front of the mirror. You're ready to make a video, but before you hit record, there are four things to consider to make sure what you make meets some basic quality requirements. Skip these steps at your peril, because no one likes a poorly made video.

Shoot it

Most current smartphones shoot high-quality 4K footage, so you probably have all the camera you need already in your hand. If you want something more professional, look into a DSLR camera, but get ready to spend some extra cash on accessories such as a microphone, as most don't come with this built in. A top tip is to look at pawn shops, second-hand stores and online listings. Lots of people spend the cash to get a DSLR only to find themselves not using it enough to justify keeping it, so you can score a deal this way.

Go steady

Shaky footage is bad footage. Get yourself a tripod (three legs) or monopod (one leg) so that you can mount your camera and get a nice steady shot. Tripods and monopods are reasonably priced and easily available online. You can even get some cool ones that wrap around things, can be hand-held, turn into selfie sticks and more.

Get lit

You can get away with natural light if you can complete filming your videos before the sun changes location, especially if you're always shooting at the same time of day, but investing in some simple lighting is a good idea so that you can ensure your videos are consistently lit. You can rig something up with a few lamps stolen from around the house, or you can invest in the YouTuber's dream lighting rig: the Ring Light. These make everyone look good. Even you.

Huh? What?

Many people forget the need for good-quality audio, but frankly it's more important than anything else. If your audio sucks, people will immediately stop watching. Test things out first when you're shooting to make sure you're getting good audio. It can be as simple as making sure you're in a quiet room, but if the audio is not to your liking, invest in a good microphone to connect to your camera. You'll get hauled over the coals in the comments if your audio is no good.

Be controversial

/JUSTDESTINY
JustDestiny
Subscribers: > 1.7m

Favourite YouTubers:
/PowerfulJRE
/BGFilms
/H3Podcast

My channel is controversial. I make videos because I want to, and I'll talk about topics that some people might avoid, especially due to demonetization (where your videos can be disqualified from earning a share of the advertising revenue due to their content). If I'm talking about a specific creator, they and their fans might be offended, but it's subjective. Some people find it hilarious. Some topics are more controversial than others, and I find that depends on what I'm talking about – whether it's a political rant or commentary about people on the platform – and how – whether it's scripted or not. If it's gonna hurt someone's feelings, I'll say it regardless. I'm not afraid to offend people; it makes me stand out. I try to tie in humour, too. I don't even think of myself as a YouTuber, I'm a content creator.

JustDestiny's story

I started as a gaming channel playing *Destiny*, but when I realized it wasn't working for me, I decided to change. I started making social commentary videos where I give opinions on lots of topics. One I made about Jake Paul reached a bigger audience, so I made more videos like that about people such as Danielle Bregoli and Woah Vicky. Things grew from there. I've worked hard, dedicating a few years to YouTube. It took me years to hit success.

「Nusa Penida」

/LOSTLEBLANC
Christian LeBlanc
Subscribers: > 1.1m

Favourite YouTubers:
/PewDiePie
/Codyko69
/sxePhil (Philip DeFranco)

Make it relatable

I focus on relatability – what my audience wants and how I can both entertain and inspire. I want viewers to feel part of my journey, so much so that they want to grab their backpack and head out that day. My core audience loves raw travel adventure, so I concentrate on budget backpacker-style travel. I ask myself, 'Could this be them in my shoes?' to help me make truly relatable videos. Make a commitment to your audience to always think about how they can relate to your content.

Christian's story

I did a semester on exchange in Thailand while studying commerce. I wanted to keep the memories, so I videoed my travels using a GoPro, knowing that soon I'd be in a 9–5 job. After about five months, what had started as a hobby with a few dozen fans grew to about 2,000 people who were interested in what it's like to be a backpacker student in Asia. I got a job in accounting, but quit after three months. I ended my apartment lease early, sold my possessions and bought a one-way ticket to Thailand. I knocked on hostel doors bartering videos for accommodation, and in six months I'd hit 50,000 subscribers. Today I make inspiring travel content that tells my story of entrepreneurship.

Don't speak

We are accepted around the world because we don't use any dialogue. It's the purest form of comedy; it's physical, not relying on telling a joke, but rather showing a joke. These universally accessible videos don't work for every YouTuber – it does depend on what you want to do – but it's something to consider. You can be massively popular speaking a language and creating content for a specific group of people, or you can look for a way to broaden your reach and appeal to a bigger audience by using visuals more than dialogue.

Buttered Side Down's story

We're filmmakers first, but we'd always wanted to have a YouTube channel so that we could entertain a large audience, try out more ideas and deliver projects quicker. When we made a short film, it took a year, whereas with YouTube there's a goalpost every two weeks, so you get the payoff sooner. We use YouTube to enable us to have creative success as quickly as possible, validating our work and proving our concepts. It's great when the rest of the world is agreeing that what we're doing is working.

/BUTTEREDSIDEDOWN
Buttered Side Down
Subscribers: > 1m

Favourite YouTubers:
/YouSuckatCooking
/CaptainDisillusion
/RedLetterMedia

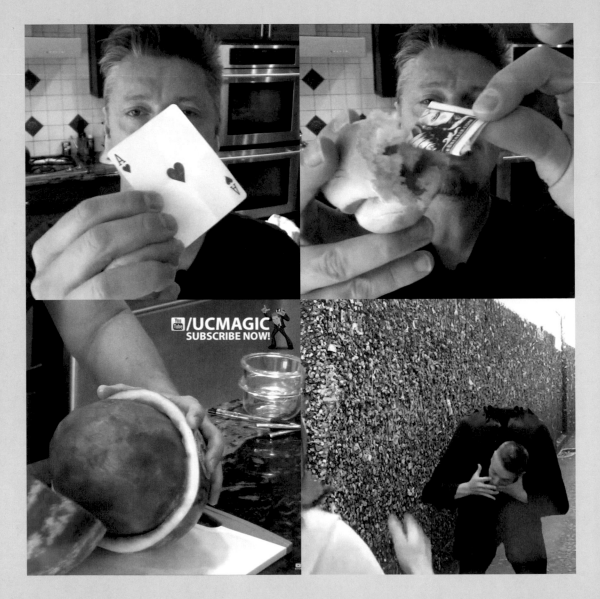

42

/RICHFERGUSON
Rich Ferguson
Subscribers: > 2.6m

Favourite YouTubers:
/AmericasGotTalent
/CoryCotton (Dude Perfect)
Anything Penn & Teller

Themes are magic

You can't make everyone happy if you spread yourself too thinly with too many different ideas for your videos and channel. You need a theme. Sure, you can make other channels if you want to diverge from your theme, but that's a lot of work. Instead, make all your videos wrap around one theme that glues everything together. For example, I make sure all my videos are about being tricky, whether I'm doing a magic trick or making a prank video. Don't dilute your efforts; instead, find the theme that connects your videos and always stick to it. That's real magic.

Rich's story

I first used YouTube to post my promotional material so that I could embed videos on my blog, but then I started to get comments asking for magic tricks and so I started making prank and magic-trick videos. In one video I scare people by taking my head off. It got 10m views overnight and quickly grew to 100m. I figured I'd try it again, so I turned on monetization and started making one video a week. I've been doing that for years now and it's been a perfect side adventure, complementing my career as a professional magician, author and speaker.

Use your YouTube voice

There really is such a thing as YouTube voice.

You've heard it a million times. YouTubers start their videos with a fun, upbeat, sing-songy voice saying 'Hey Guys! It's ME! Sorry I've not made a video in a while, life has been craaaaaazy.' And they maintain that fast-paced, perky, bubbly voice throughout the video. But why?

It turns out that this style of speaking is particularly good at getting and maintaining the attention of the audience. Using a YouTube voice is especially great if you're making a video where it's just you speaking to the camera. Straight monologues are boring if you don't up the ante, so try the following:

Bring the energy

Whatever you're saying, say it with energy. People want to watch videos that you wanted to make, so if they think you're not into it, why should they be? Before you hit record, psych yourself up to raise your energy level. Jog on the spot, look in the mirror and tell yourself you're awesome, do whatever you like to get in the zone. When you hit record, you should be ON and ready to hit the ground running. Kick things off with energy and maintain it all the time you're recording. You only get to turn off when the camera is off.

Emphasize it

You can overstress your words, stretch them out, dial your volume up and down, and find lots of ways to play with your words to create emphasis. You should emphasize words to grab the listener's attention; just watch some of the YouTubers in this book and you'll quickly see how they modify the way they speak. You'll get attention and maintain it if you play with emphasis, whereas keeping things monotone is a sure-fire way to turn people off.

Pace to win the race

Combine energy and emphasis with pace for a winning formula. Your pace is the speed with which you're speaking. You can speed things up, slow things down or maintain a consistently fast pace throughout. Quick cuts help you cut out dead air (see the technical tangent on editing tips, pp. 56–7, for more on this) and keep the pace up. It also makes it easier to record your videos, because you can shoot your video in short bursts, editing it together at the end.

Maximize evergreen videos

Helpful evergreen content is always at the top of my list. You'll rarely see a video from me that's a current trend or something seasonally specific. For example, I won't say 'My Favourite Fall Recipes', I'll say 'My Favourite Slow Cooker Recipes' so that people will click on it all year round. You can refer to your evergreen videos all year long because they are always relevant; if you make videos based on trends you'll get a few extra clicks in the moment, but miss out on the long-term play. So, make your videos evergreen, and you'll maximize your click potential all year.

Jordan's story

I started back in 2011 with a blog, and occasionally put videos on YouTube that I could then post to the blog and my social channels. Flash forward a few years and it had become my fastest-growing, most effective and most engaged platform. I make videos about frugal living, style, budgeting, productivity and my life as a wife and mother. I've always put family first, so I had to get really particular about being productive and working smarter, not harder. I film and edit for maybe two hours a day, four days a week, so it's manageable while I balance life with my husband, Bubba, and our six kids.

/FUNCHEAPORFREE
Jordan Page
Subscribers: > 560k

Favourite YouTubers:
/TheBucketListFamily
/BadLipReading
/MyChicLife (Rachel Hollis)

1: BUY IN BULK

/HOTBANANASTUD
Brandon Rogers
Subscribers: > 5m

Favourite YouTubers:
/DailyDoseofInternet
/HowToBasic
/ShootYourMouthOffFilms

Collect your cavalcade of characters

When you meet someone who sounds or looks weird, or is interesting or gorgeous or disgusting or stands out in some other way, don't let them go. Create your cavalcade of characters and use them in your videos. I went out of my way to collect a group of people who are diverse, get along and can be family. All the people I've worked with fell into my life, and now I write to their strengths. I find that on set 90 per cent of the vibe is who you are off camera, so work with a team of people whom you love and who are comfortable with one another.

Brandon's story

At school, we'd make sketch videos and play them at the video club. It was the first time I'd heard someone laugh at something I'd made. I loved it – it was the ultimate high. For ten years I made and posted videos to YouTube. One day I woke up to a text from a friend telling me my channel had blown up. The Fine Bros had made a video about me, and that opened the floodgates. All those years I thought I was wasting my life, but when everyone was sent over to my channel there was years of material, which helped the channel blast off overnight.

Break it to remake it

/THEKINGOFRANDOM
Grant Thompson
Subscribers: > 11.4m

Favourite YouTubers:
/KipKay
/HouseholdHacker
/TheBackyardScientist

If your content starts to feel stale, it's OK to shake things up. You should never be afraid of making a change. We've had the most success when switching things up that at first might feel like a mistake, but turned out to be exactly the right thing to do. Sure, major change is hard, but in the end it always creates more growth. Try to detach yourself emotionally and say to yourself, 'Here's the right thing to do and I'm gonna do it.' Don't hold yourself back.

Grant's story

I've driven school buses, worked on oil rigs, been a pilot and worked in real estate, but now I have a team of 14 people working on my YouTube channel and I'm semi-retired. We make five videos a week, born out of my quest to figure out how things work. I take pride in breaking complex things down into their simple components. A friend would call me the King of Random because I always had something new to show him that I'd been experimenting with. My videos encapsulate the idea that you can make anything with anything.

Grant Thompson passed away during the production of this book. His team have set up the Grant Thompson Memorial Outward Bound Scholarship, and encourage fans of the channel to do a random act of love or kindness in his honour.

Commit to the process

Don't assume that you as a human being aren't good enough because someone dislikes your video. Just because someone dislikes my video doesn't mean they dislike me. I use every video as an opportunity to see how I can make the content better. Disconnect yourself from dislikes and instead revise your methodology. You must commit to the process: your focus should be about making the best piece of content you possibly can.

Casually Explained's story

While I was at university studying engineering I decided to make videos on topics such as calculus to motivate me to get through the courses. I made one video that was a long joke, which I posted on a sub-Reddit. It got cross-posted and had 300,000 views overnight. I thought maybe I could do this again, and was able to keep repeating the success. It really seemed to be something, so I dropped out after my first year of college to pursue YouTube ... I guess the thing I started to keep me in school led to me dropping out!

Say yes

The advice we give to anyone who says they aspire to have a channel like ours is: SAY YES. We believe strongly in serendipity. When you start a YouTube channel, the universe will magically conspire to put things in front of you or move things out of your way. Say yes to them. Say yes to serendipity and to trying new things, even when you don't think it'll lead anywhere. Our most popular video, about an abandoned city with no laws, nearly didn't get made because we weren't sure people would watch it. We said yes, and it has 18m views and counting. Even if you're hesitant, say yes. You might be surprised at the way things turn out.

Yes Theory's story

We bonded over challenging ourselves to do 30 things in 30 days, making a video each day. Even if it went nowhere, it'd be fun and make a great story. When it was over, we'd never been happier and had got around 10,000 subscribers. Then a studio in Venice, California, asked if we wanted to move there and make content for them. We said yes. We kept working on our YouTube channel, which became Yes Theory. We've been saying yes ever since and our audience is now over 4.3m subscribers.

/PRACPROCRASTINATION
Yes Theory
Subscribers: > 4.3m

Favourite YouTubers:
/DanTheDirector1
(Dan Mace)
/AndreasAHem
/ColinandSamir

It's a reel job

You can edit your videos to cut out all those moments when you messed up, speed up the pace, tweak the audio, add graphics, whatever you need to do to make your video feel more polished. Basic editing is easy to learn. Here are some tips to get you started.

Back it up, baby

OK, so you've shot your footage and you're ready to edit away. Before you do anything, back it up. You want to have a complete unedited, original copy of your footage somewhere, such as on a hard drive or memory card or in the cloud. Then you'll always have it handy if you need it. Losing this footage means shooting the whole thing from scratch if something goes wrong.

Choose your tool

Most laptops and computers come with some kind of editing software already loaded. For example, Macs usually have iMovie pre-installed. If you want a pro tool, check out Adobe Premiere CC or Final Cut Pro.

Refine, refine, refine

A lot of people make a rough cut of their video first, and then refine it later. Watch through your footage and work out which bits grab your attention and which bits have you dozing off. Then watch it through again and think about your original intention for the video. If your divergence is funny or interesting, keep it, but try to keep the message of the video clear and succinct.

Graphic content

Depending on what your video is about, try adding graphics. YouTubers ranting on a topic might throw in funny visuals that match what they are saying. It helps to keep people's attention and adds to the richness of your video, making it more than just you talking to camera.

Try fast cuts

Fast cuts, or quick cuts, is a popular editing technique with YouTubers. Let's say you're speaking directly to camera in a ten-minute Zombie Taco Halloween costume makeup tutorial. When you're editing, you'll cut out any moments of silence, pauses, 'errs' and 'umms' to make the whole thing feel quicker-paced. It's popular because it keeps the viewer's attention.

Get help

Practice makes perfect, so stick with it, but if you're not good at editing you can get help from online services like Fiverr. Most popular YouTubers end up employing someone to edit their videos, because it takes so much time.

So nice you could do it twice

/PLANETDOLAN
/SUPERPLANETDOLAN
/THEDDGUIDES
Planet Dolan
Subscribers: > 5.8m
        > 1.8m
        > 1.1m

Favourite YouTubers:
/Penguinz0
/FilmCourage
/VideoCreatorsTV

My first channel was a gaming channel, and my second featured educational videos about the real world using animations. If you want to make videos that are very different from what you've done before, consider creating a second channel. Some fans will come over, some won't. It's interesting to figure out how you're going to manage several channels at once, and being able to reinvent yourself is quite nice, although it's easy to overstretch yourself.

Planet Dolan's story

I got some funding from an Australian self-employment course that helped me pump out lots of gaming videos as experiments to find what worked best. Education videos, especially lists, worked well and helped my channel to take off. I kept on experimenting and started a second channel where I use animation and education together.

Make it visual

It's really important to have strong, appealing visual content. YouTube is a visual medium. As soon as I finish writing a song, I think about how it could look in a video. When you get an idea for a video and start to piece things together, think about being as visual as possible. I like to focus on one small element: for example, for my song 'Tamale', I might dissect the concept of a tamale to make it appealing in a video. You can make things visual by exploring and taking advantage of the magic in ordinary moments.

Daniela's story

I got started on YouTube after catching the wave of Nexopia and MySpace. People were creating profiles and learning how to code. My friends and I would hang out in front of a camera, tell jokes, make sketches, play them back and laugh. I posted a video covering a Michael Bublé song and it got 10,000 views, which was big back then. Things just happened after that. Now, I follow my instinct when choosing songs to cover. It's a raw feeling that something might be great. My Radiohead and Gnarls Barkley covers changed the course of my life and career. I relocated to a bigger city, and now I'm moving out of covers to be part of the music industry in a more traditional, tangible way.

/DANIELASINGS
Daniela Andrade
Subscribers: > 1.7m

Favourite YouTubers:
/ClothesEncounters (Jenn Im)
/COLORS
/NPRMusic

GENESIS

DANIELA ANDRADE

/ONISION
/ONISIONSPEAKS
/UHOHBRO

Onision
Subscribers: > 2m
> 2m
> 2m

Favourite YouTubers:
/NathanJBarnatt
/Laineybot
/HotBananaStud (Brandon Rogers)

Collaborate

Don't rely only on the algorithm, because it changes often and you can lose your whole career overnight. The consistent thing I've seen work time and time again is knowing and working with the right people. Connect with other YouTubers and ask to work with them. Get creative with how you work across different channels. For example, I would make videos with alternative endings that people could find on different channels. Make friends with famous YouTubers and your channel will explode.

Onision's story

I'd been making videos while I was in the Air Force stationed in South Korea. Back in 2007, I started out with the Onision channel with opinion, music and comedy sketch videos. YouTube sometimes featured me on the homepage, and one day I got 750,000 views on a video. That increased my subscribers, and my channel started to thrive. I eventually split the channels, creating Onision Speaks and UhOhBro to separate the videos, because some people want the opinion videos but not the comedy and vice versa.

Run it like a company

I manage a team of people to make sure we hit our deadlines. I'll write a script, get voice actors to record it, tell the team of animators what to draw, and have another team write video captions. I even have a person who edits my videos for other platforms, such as Facebook and Amazon. It's a big responsibility when you're in charge – if you don't work, no one else works – so you should run your channel like a company to ensure everyone is delivering.

Gizzy Gazza's story

I've been on YouTube for 11 years with my Gizzy Gazza channel, making videos simply because it was fun. When I started to make Minecraft videos in 2012, my channel began to grow, hitting around 1m subscribers within three years. I've adapted over time, but my focus today is still on gaming, now using animation. It takes about two weeks to make each video with a team of five, and I mix in some story-time videos about my personal life for fans who want to know more.

/GIZZY14GAZZA
/GIZLIFE
Gizzy Gazza
Subscribers: > 1.9m
> 45k

Favourite YouTubers:
/Pyrocynical
/PewDiePie
/Shane (Shane Dawson)

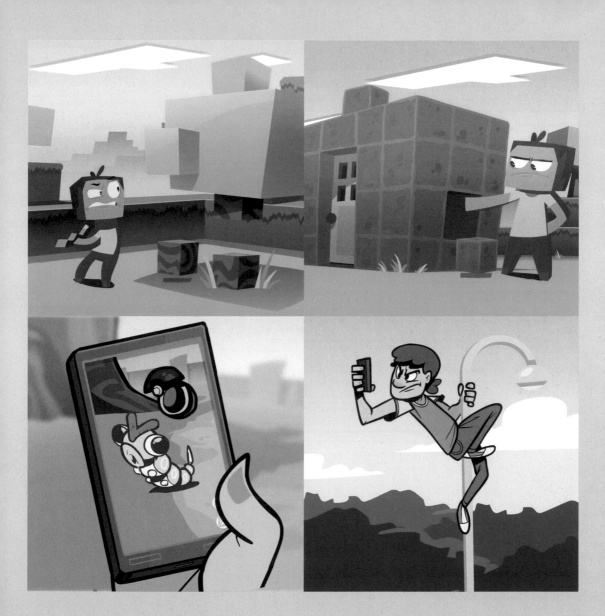

/WHEALTHBYSLAIMAN
/SLAIMANANDKATE
Kate Martineau
Subscribers: > 2.2m
> 450k

Favourite YouTubers:
/JennaMarbles
/LeFloofTV
(SACCONEJOLYs)
/ZoeSugg

Perfect the prank

Prank videos are huge on YouTube, and there's no limit to what you can do. We're a couple who prank each other; pranking a partner is easier than pranking complete strangers. Whoever you prank, make sure they are OK with everything afterwards. If they don't like it, don't post it, just ditch it. Sometimes pranks go sour, and that can be a shock. Sit down, talk and decide what to do. Pranks are fun, but you don't want to be embarrassed in a video that goes too far. As long as you're in tune with each other, you'll be OK. If not, you'll break up.

Kate's story

Slaiman, my boyfriend, was a fan of Prank vs. Prank, and one day he pranked me. I didn't take it well. I didn't want to be one of those people constantly getting pranked in YouTube videos, but he showed me the video, I told him his editing sucked, and he posted it. When he kept making prank videos I slowly warmed to the idea, and started to prank him back. I had the idea for a 'how many pranks can you fit into one day' video that made our channel take off. People know that although we're always annoying each other, there's a solid foundation of trust and love, so it's never mean-spirited.

Video over?
Explain what to do next

When you make your video, always use the last 5–20 seconds as an 'end screen'. You'll have seen these on videos you've watched; they encourage the viewer to watch more or to take some kind of action. Here are some ideas for what to include on your end screen.

'Watch this video'

Call out or link to one of your other videos or playlists. Ideally, it'll be a video that makes sense as something to watch next, perhaps a follow-up or related video.

'Check out this channel'

Let viewers know if you have another YouTube channel or if you want them to check out a friend's channel.

'Don't forget to subscribe'

Always ask viewers to subscribe to your channel, to help guarantee that they come back to watch more of your videos later.

'Visit my website'

You can promote your website, social media, or other sites, such as a crowdfunding campaign.

'Buy the new T-shirt'

Link viewers to your online swag store so they can buy your coffee mug and T-shirt.

Pro tip!

When you get invited to special programmes run by YouTube, you often get access to extra features that let you boost the functionality of things like your end screen.

Choreograph the shot

/HEVESH5
Lily Hevesh
Subscribers: > 2.5m

Favourite YouTubers:
/CaseyNeistat
/llSuperwomanll
/ThisIsSmileyandShell
(Michelle Reed)

There's an art to filming my domino videos, because it's a one-take shot. After it's over, did it even happen? You have to plan ahead, place your tripods strategically to capture when you're building the setup and for all your trick shots. Everything is choreographed, and that's as important as the action itself. I don't hire a cameraperson, as they have no idea how to film what I'm doing. With any video, you must learn to choreograph, plan ahead and make sure you get the shots you need, if you want to tell the story successfully.

Lily's story

When I was nine I loved setting up and knocking down my dominoes. I searched YouTube and found people who had set dominoes up, so I could just watch them fall down! I became obsessed, and watched virtually every domino video on YouTube in 2009. I was so inspired, I *needed* to get more dominoes to start posting on YouTube and be part of that community. I learned new tricks and my videos kept growing. More people found them and I got comments from builders everywhere. It's an odd hobby, but I shared it with many other people worldwide. The comments motivated me to keep posting and building, and now I'm doing YouTube full-time.

/PRESTONPLAYZ

Preston
Subscribers: > 10.6m

Favourite YouTubers:
/xJawz
/Tobuscus
/Matroix (Ali-A)

Do your research

Time spent researching is time well spent. I pick out 50 YouTube channels at a time and research them, asking myself, 'Why are they getting views? What are they doing? How are they separating themselves from the pack? What's their secret sauce?' Often the simplest answer is the right one. Don't copy them, but make them your own. Just digest as much YouTube content as you can so you really live and breathe it. You must spend the hours researching, digging through and finding the works of art that are producing so much fruit.

Preston's story

I had built up about 100k subscribers playing *Call of Duty* competitively, but I wanted people to stick around for me. It gets exhausting grinding on the game, and I wanted to be like Tobuscus, with his amazing positive energy. I love the way he carries himself in videos and how his commentary flows. Now I'm expanding. Faith and family are a huge part of my business, and a driving force in my life. My mom and dad are both involved in my business operations, my wife has a channel with over 1m subscribers and my little brother features in my videos – he's even becoming his own celebrity. My future is running more businesses, using YouTube as a platform.

Find your format

/DOUGDEMURO
/MOREDOUGDEMURO
Doug DeMuro
Subscribers: > 3.1m
> 525k

Favourite YouTubers:
/HooviesGarage
/TheSmokingTire
/CaseyNeistat

You've got to find the format that works for your videos. You only start to hone the format (and make money) when you listen to what people want. It took me about a year to find the repeatable template that works for me. Now I can travel to wherever the car is, write the script, shoot the video and edit it in about five hours. People make fun of me for my intros, but I know what works; the whole point about my intros is to start with a focus on the car. You'll figure out the format that works for you.

Doug's story

Straight after college I worked at Porsche's corporate HQ in Atlanta and got a Porsche 911 as my company car. The thing is, it's really cool when you're 21, but when you're picking up your seventh 911, you think, 'Is this gonna be my whole life? Renting these cars from my employer?' I felt I could do more than sit in a cubicle and work on spreadsheets. So I quit to write about cars for Jalopnik. One day a guy emailed to say I was really funny and should make videos. It hadn't occurred to me, but each video led to the next and more than 600 million views later, here we are.

/HELLOITSAMIE
Amie
Subscribers: > 1.7m

Favourite YouTubers:
/TheAceFamily
/TheLaBrantFam
/IvoryGirl48 (Mia Maples)

Don't burn out

Creator burnout is real. Some YouTubers feel they let everyone down if they take a break from making videos, but there's no shame in that. It's a full-time job, and when you devote everything to your channel and keeping your audience happy, it's easy to get exhausted. It doesn't have the work/life balance of more traditional jobs. I've found that scheduling my content commitments reduces the risk of burnout, but you do need to keep an element of spontaneity. As soon as you feel you're forcing something, stop, because it'll be obvious to your audience. Making time to go offline can be just as important as being online. I've had some of my best ideas when taking a break.

Amie's story

When I was 11 I started using the app Video Star, which was like the original version of TikTok/Musical.ly. I posted the content on YouTube and soon started getting subscribers. It was exciting, and I quickly realized that I wanted to create more content for YouTube and express my creativity in other ways. I wanted to make videos where I could interact with the viewers, and I wanted to get to know the people who were becoming my fans and to share more of myself with them. Now I have more subscribers than I could have dreamed of! I focus on YouTube because it has a special place in my journey as a creator.

Create. Curate. Collaborate.

Being a YouTuber is all about creating videos, but you've got a few options when it comes to how to make videos for your channel, beyond just hitting record. Consider creating, curating and collaborating.

Create

YouTubers create their own videos, and most start out by recording, editing and publishing themselves. As you become more successful, consider enlisting the help of others for your video creation. Maybe you need a friend to help capture the footage when you're out shooting on the street, or to help you edit all your footage together (editing takes a lot of time). If you need something that you can't convince a buddy to help with, you can get help from online platforms such as Fiverr. You can enlist the services of people for animations and graphics, editing, sound work and more, all for reasonable prices.

Curate

Did you know that you can curate other people's content? Just make playlists of other people's videos as a way to build your own channel. This is especially handy if other people are making videos that you love, and that are relevant to your work, but that you wouldn't make yourself. Let's say you're a beauty vlogger, but you don't make videos about the use of prosthetics in makeup. Why not curate a playlist of your favourite prosthetic tutorials by other YouTubers? Your fans will love that you've done the work of finding awesome videos for them. Playlists appear in YouTube's search results, so you might snag subscribers to your channel without even needing to create more videos.

Collaborate

You'll see all the biggest YouTube stars collaborating with one another. It's a great way to create more content for your channel, with the added benefit of tapping into other people's audiences. They'll send subscribers to your channel and vice versa. It's a proven method for growing fans, and it's a great way to engage in the YouTuber community. So, find someone you like and reach out to them through their channel to suggest that you collaborate. It's best to have an idea of how your partnership would work – so pitch them your best ideas as to why they should work with you.

Attract attention immediately

In the first five seconds you've got to attract the viewer's attention. We show close-ups of our cakes to grab people right out of the gate, rather than taking 30 seconds slowly getting into the video. Sometimes the cake doesn't even look as though it could possibly be a cake. It's like, 'You wanna see a cake that looks like a human heart? Sure you do.' A strong visual is a huge advantage if you want to capture attention and encourage people to stick around and watch more, so find the image that will help you to attract attention immediately.

Yolanda, Jocelyn and Connie's story

The three of us have collaborated to build up our channel. Yolanda is the face of the brand and Chief Cake Officer, and Connie and Jocelyn create the strategy and drive the business. We all worked in TV, but our big driver for getting on YouTube was freedom to make the content we wanted to make without having to ask permission. We got really fatigued going through all the steps, people and hoops in TV. So we invested as a team in How To Cake It, knowing that we all have different strengths and we all contribute. That's what makes us so strong. What's next? World domination, of course.

/HOWTOCAKEIT
/HOWTOCAKEITSTEPBYSTEP

Connie Contardi
Jocelyn Mercer
Yolanda Gampp
Subscribers: > 4m
                  > 280k

Favourite YouTubers:
Connie: /BigThink
Jocelyn: /ItsKingsleyBitch (Kingsley)
Yolanda: /sxePhil (Philip DeFranco)

/VAT19
Vat19
Subscribers: > 6.4m

Favourite YouTubers:
/DrawWithJazza
/TheKingofRandom
/SongsToWearPantsTo
(Andrew Huang)

Promote a product, but make it entertaining

You can make money promoting products, but most people want to skip commercials. You've got to make your ads entertaining so that people will want to watch. Look at our channel: it's all ads for products we sell, but we have over 5.8m subscribers who are effectively saying, 'Please interrupt my day with a new commercial.' The real test is when people finish watching a video and think 'Did I just watch a commercial?' Just make sure you love the product too. Oh, and if you can get laughs, you can sell anything.

Vat19's story

I had a video production company in St Louis, making TV commercials for local companies. I loved making commercials, but hated the job. We weren't making much money, so I thought it would be cool to make commercials the way we wanted, to have fun, and no clients telling us what to do. I figured the only way would be to have the store where we sold the products. We posted videos of products on YouTube just as a hosting solution, but some went nuts. One called 'Das Beer Boot' has an unbelievable 21m views now. Our video for the world's largest gummy worm ended up on the trending page – that has 84m views.

Try Instagram first

It might seem counterintuitive, but you can start off making videos for Instagram before making the transition to YouTube. It can be easier to be discovered and increase your fanbase through Instagram, thanks to hashtags and the Explore page. You can also experiment with what works there, before you make a plan for the videos you'll make on YouTube.

Jessica's story

I started off on Instagram, where I focused on uploading photos of my makeup transformations. Soon my fanbase was big enough that fans also wanted tutorials on YouTube, so I began the channel and things took off from there. My most popular video is my Betty Boop transformation, which has 26m views. The channel itself has over 1.6m subscribers, plus another 270,000 subscribers on my Jessica Vill channel, where I make videos about vintage fashion and makeup, along with my adventures.

/JBUNZIE
/JESSICAVILL
Jessica Vill
Subscribers: > 1.6m
> 270k

Inspiration:
Documentaries
Music
Anything vintage

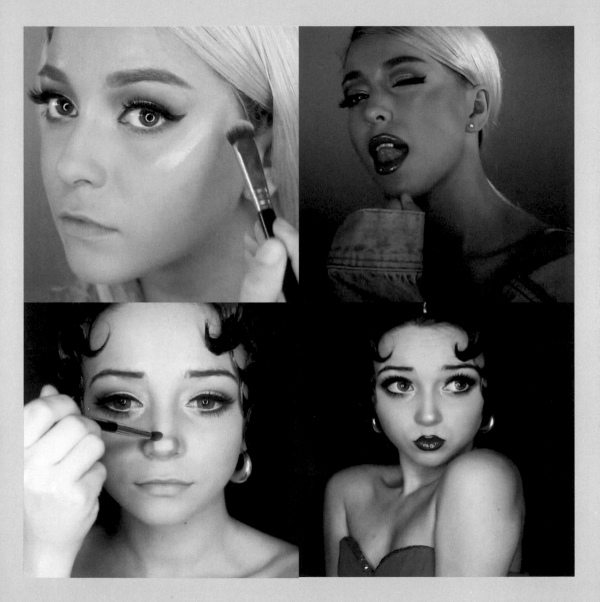

Listen to your gut

/TOYOTALAUREN
Lauren Toyota
Subscribers: > 157k

Favourite YouTubers:
/trickNiks (Nikki Limo)
/TheFightingSolo (Julien Solomita)
/TheLateLateShowwithJamesCorden

Letting people into your life is where the momentum can start. They will connect with you more because they like the way you really are, but set your boundary by listening to your intuition. If you record something and it feels wrong or weird in your gut when you watch it, don't post it. The need to share is helpful but sometimes harmful, and it's easy to overshare. Sure, put it out there, but always take care of yourself. Keep something for yourself, create outwards but don't cross your line. Ask yourself, 'Am I creating for me or am I creating for you?' You need both, in balance.

Lauren's story

I didn't think YouTube was a legitimate platform. I started my channel because my career at MTV had halted. I had started a food blog and Instagram, but it took me about a year to get the urge to create videos. I was apprehensive at first, and wasn't sure what I was getting into, despite having a background in production. There wasn't any cool, slick, mainstream vegan food content, and I thought I could offer something different, something inspired and culinary. Now I use video to shine a light on veganism in the way that I feel it deserves.

Getting found

No one knows all the secrets of the YouTube algorithm, that magic formula of code that decides which videos to serve up where and when, but YouTube does give you all the clues you need to make sure you maximize your chances of discovery. When you upload your video, make sure you use all these features to increase your exposure.

Write the right title

A great title is key. Make it accurate, succinct and compelling, only including what's really important. Your title is your chance to state clearly what your video is about, a big signal to help the algorithm decide whether to serve your video up when someone searches. Check out AsapSCIENCE (see p.114) for a masterclass in effective title writing.

Tag it

Tags probably aren't the most important factor in getting found, but they are still a feature that YouTube includes when you're uploading your video, so it's best to take advantage. Write at least 20 tags using keywords that accurately describe what your video is about and that match what people are most likely to be looking for.

A full description

A great description is key, especially the first few lines, which display in YouTube's search results and which people use when deciding if yours is the video they should click on. Write at least 100 words describing what your video is about. A good description will get straight to the point but be comprehensive, and should include links to anything you mention in your video, plus links to your social profiles. Take a look at Jordan Page's channel (see p.46) for great examples of video descriptions.

Closed captions and transcripts

You can add closed captions to your videos – the subtitles that display what's being said in the video – which are great for people who want to watch the video with sound off. The extra benefit is that they give YouTube clues about the content of your video. You can also add a transcript, a complete write-up of everything said in the video, to the description.

Add it to a playlist

Always add your videos to playlists, because playlists are shown in the search results. It's like having another ticket in the lottery: each playlist gives you an extra chance of being found.

Actions are signals

Sure, you'll be asking people to comment, subscribe and share, and beyond the obvious benefits these are signals that YouTube probably uses to move you up the search rankings. If people are commenting lots on a particular video, it might be served up more to people searching.

Search and you will find

Type something into the YouTube search bar and you'll see it autofill to show you what other people are interested in. Then all you need to do is make videos for those search terms. For example, 'how to jump rope ... like a boxer ... for weight loss ... for beginners'. It's as though YouTube gives you the playbook for what you should make and what's going to do well. There are other tools out there that can score search terms for how much traffic they get and whether they are competitive or not. As your channel grows, you can compete for more popular searches.

Brandon and Dan's story

Dan had lost a lot of weight jumping rope, and Brandon had his own fitness coaching company. We decided to combine the two, so we quit everything, moved to Colombia (it's more affordable there) and started making videos. We made close to 200, but didn't break 1,000 subscribers in a year. We had no traction and were running out of money, but then one video exploded: 'How to jump rope like a boxer.' That set the tone for the rest of our growth. After a few years we moved to Los Angeles, and now we focus on keeping our content entertaining, fresh and relevant. There's a lot more we can do.

/JUMPROPEDUDES
Brandon Epstein
Dan Witmer
Subscribers: > 475k

Favourite YouTubers:
Brandon:
/GaryVaynerchuk (Gary Vee)

Dan:
/PeterMcKinnon24
/PewDiePie
/Henbu

Shoot overhead

I could shoot overhead videos all day long. You can use overhead videos to showcase your creative ideas and projects, bringing them to life in a well-edited video that's easy to make, and the best part is that you don't even need to put on makeup. Just make sure you have a decent manicure and that your hands are clean. I find you get fewer negative comments with this format because you're focusing on the project, rather than being on camera yourself. You do need the right setup, though. There are wonderful tripods that sit on your desk (mine is from Arkon Mounts), and you'll also need a ring light and a soft box.

Amy's story

When I started on YouTube, I was already creating content as a full-time scrapbooker, evolving into a lifestyle brand mainly through Instagram, sharing what I was doing with like-minded creatives. YouTube is one of the ways I take people on my travels around the world. I experience cool adventures and then come back into the studio, showing people how I document everything in albums and scrapbooks. The more we share about our journeys, the more people feel positively affected by change, so I hope to continue to inspire people to get creative and to live their best creative life.

/AMYTANGERINE
Amy Tangerine
Subscribers: > 50k

Favourite YouTubers:
/HowtoCakeIt
/MarieForleo
/JenniferMcGuireInk

/KINGVADER
King Vader
Subscribers: > 1.6m

Favourite YouTubers:
/TheRackaRacka
/WolfGraphic
/GizzlyB3aver (CalebCity)

Drop a season

You can drop a bunch of videos in one go, instead of busting out a video every day. I make collections of videos, like a musician making an album, creating content and packaging it as though it's a big album drop. That way you can take your time, which helps you make high-quality content instead of getting caught in the trap of quantity. I'd rather deliver 5 amazing videos than 30 average ones. You'll find that people love going to your channel and realizing there are these deep collections of videos to watch, and they will see that you put 100 per cent effort into everything, not just some of your videos.

King Vader's story
My cousin (who is now my manager) brought me into this world when he wanted me to be in his videos. At first I was unsure, but I started to enjoy it. Vine came out, and I hopped on there. That's how I developed my own unique style and found my own path. I started to get followers – people believed in me – but then Vine shut down, so I pushed really hard on Instagram and YouTube, and now we've got more than a million followers and subscribers. My future is about directing and acting. I want to be one of those rare people in my generation who do both. I want to be the best.

5 THINGS NOT TO BUY AT WAL-MART

/THEDEALGUY
Matt Granite
Subscribers: > 555k

Favourite YouTubers:
/EpicMealTime
/JimmyKimmelLive
/MadilynBailey

Reward your core audience

Don't do what I did, and spend $20,000 in postage giving away freebies. All I gained was a bunch of teenagers who won't buy anything but who got a free used blender. Sure, create an incentive for people to watch, but identify the core audience who specifically want to watch your videos, and reward them. The 2,000 people who love you, your message and the blender you're featuring, and who will buy that blender, are worth more than the 20,000 watching without buying, just skipping ahead to win your giveaway. Giveaways are meant to reward core viewers, not incentivize new subscribers.

Matt's story

I developed a TV show on bargain hunting, but my family complained that they weren't around when it was on, or didn't get the channel. My wife suggested I put videos on YouTube. When the TV network told me it owned the content and I should stop, I knew I was on the brink of something. I searched for help, found Studio71 and convinced their receptionist to put me through to someone high up (John Carle, see p.120). They were so dumbfounded by this that I got a talent manager, Matthew, who has taught me a huge amount about YouTube. Now the TV network embraces what I do. And instead of doing giveaways, I take the products to homeless shelters.

THE
BEVERLY HILLS BRAT

CHAMPS
11:03PM

RITE AID
2:43AM

9:30AM

/NICOLETTEGRAY
Nicolette Gray
The Beverly Hills Brat
Subscribers: > 1.1m

Favourite YouTubers:
/TanaMongeau
/NikiandGabiBeauty
/EdgarMcSteelPotCo
(Tanner Braungardt)

Challenge yourself

Make a challenge video! My manager and I look at YouTube to see what other people are doing to brainstorm together. Write a list of challenges you could do, and talk about how to morph the video to fit your brand. Make sure you keep the balance between your core content, which for me is reality drama, and the number of challenge videos you make. The YouTube community really love challenge videos because they see people, like our family, coming together to do things they normally wouldn't do. We've made videos where we wear really long nails, live on $10 a day, do a 24-hour shopping challenge and more.

Nicolette's story

I appeared on the TV show *Dr Phil*, which brought me a lot of publicity. I'd been making videos for YouTube for years, but after the show I saw a real business opportunity and took it. My years of experience meant I was prepared to take advantage of the opportunity. I now create videos consistently, involving my family, and it's brought us closer together. I'm in it for the long haul, so the goal now is to grow fast but avoid burnout.

No comment

You should know that the comments on YouTube can be pretty dark and miserable. Some people love to be negative, mean-spirited and downright rude, and when you're making videos it's best to have a plan in place so that you're prepared to handle comments, otherwise they can get you down. Having said that, it's not all bad. Your fans will heap on the praise, telling you what they love and what they want to see more of, and listening to them can uncover gold to help you increase both fans and views.

Reward your fans

Check your comments regularly, and be sure to like, heart and reply to comments as much as possible. Your fans want to interact with you, so in your videos, ask them what they think or what they want to see more of – anything that allows them a chance to contribute. Take a look at some of your favourite YouTubers to see how they encourage their fans to comment.

Don't feed the trolls

If you reply, you feed the troll and make them stronger, so if someone is being a dick, just don't engage. They are baiting you, wanting you to get upset or angry, so ignoring them is the best course of action. If you really must engage, rise above it and be the better person. Be polite and kind, address the facts, keep it short and sweet, and resist the temptation to call them out for being a garbage human being. They are garbage, and living their life is their punishment.

Need help? Enlist a friend

If you're having a hard time with comments, why not have someone else read them for you? Sam from This Exists (see p.12) has his wife, Ashley, read all his comments and only tell him the ones that help him to make his videos better. She leaves out all the nonsense that isn't helpful. It's an easy way for him to stay sane and keep the trolls at bay.

Keep it clean

/NICKDROSSOS
/CODEREDDEFENSETV
/HAVETHEBALLSTOTALK
 ABOUTIT

Nick Drossos
Subscribers: > 380k
            > 205k
            > 218

Favourite YouTubers:
/KerwinRae
/GaryVaynerchuk (GaryVee)

You've got to clean up your act. In my first YouTube videos, every second word is F&*K and B&*^H – and there's even aggressive language like 'Smash his face'. People told me to clean it up, because that's the only way to be taken seriously. If you don't, you look trashy and unprofessional. You don't need to swear and scream to get your message across, so sharpen up, clean up your language, your attitude, your image, and you'll appeal to more people. You might just find that YouTube helps you grow as a person. It did for me.

Nick's story

It was my dream to be an actor, but it can be hard to make it, and easy to feel discouraged. I was teaching self-defence, and I decided to open my own YouTube channel, do what I love and teach people self-defence in a way that's also entertaining. I started out knowing nothing, just posting videos, but things grew. People wrote to me saying they wanted to see more, so I started to build the channel by learning about what works. Now I also host a men's talk show with a doctor, where we talk about men's issues that normally don't get discussed. Not bad for a high-school dropout.

NICK DROSSOS

SELF DEFENSE, FITNESS AND LIFE COACH

YEAH, I AIN'T HAD TO BAKE FOR A GIRL IN A LONG TIME

I THINK MY COOKING'S AWESOME

I HURT THE GINGERBREAD BOY

CUZ HE'S PRETEND-BREAD BOY

NO ONE WANTED YOUR STINKING TIARA

I JUST LIKE TO DANCE!

/BADLIPREADING
Bad Lip Reading
Subscribers: > 7.4m

Favourite YouTubers:
/CaseyNeistat
/Vsauce
/schmoyoho

Please yourself first

I don't follow any of the standard guidelines for YouTube success. The best advice I can give is: 'Please yourself first.' You can't appeal to everyone, so focus on making content that you yourself respond to, and trust that like-minded people will find it. The few times I've made content for other reasons, the results have been mixed. I live for those moments when I realize that even if everybody on the planet hated what I'm working on, my satisfaction wouldn't be affected. I've had a few videos that didn't perform that well, but which I'm proud of. That satisfaction pushes me to make videos that are more successful. Let the joy you feel during the execution be most of your reward.

Bad Lip Reading's story

My mother lost her hearing in her forties, and became amazing at lip reading. I would mute the TV to see what her world was like, but I was terrible at it. Later I was reviewing silent footage from a shoot I had just been on, and it looked as though one of the people said 'bacon hobbit'. I recorded those words over the video and sent it to some friends, who thought it was hilarious and asked me to do more. So I started my channel, simply as a way to share longer videos with friends. That's when I created the phrase 'bad lip reading' to describe these kinds of videos. They sent the links to their friends, and I had an audience. But it was really the joy of making my friends laugh that made me create the channel. And that translated to a wider audience.

Keep going, no matter what

YouTube is a long game. You have to be patient and persevere indefinitely, because nothing is guaranteed. Most people give up because they don't see the results they want in the time they set for themselves. Failure happens only when you give up. If you keep trying and you're smart about it – learning and improving – you'll find your voice, your niche and, eventually, success. But you have to be willing to work for years without reward, and you can't predict when things will take off. That's where the patience comes in. Keep creating, and eventually it'll happen.

Aileen's story

In high school, I started a YouTube channel in secret. I loved to sing and play the piano, but I was too shy to tell anyone. I felt more comfortable sharing my music with strangers. Eventually, everyone found out, and I continued throughout college. After graduating I had no idea what to do, so for two years I pursued various things. I read self-help books trying to figure out my purpose. I learned so much that I started a new channel, Lavendaire, to share it all. It was hard to find young people talking about personal growth on YouTube, but I knew there must be other recent grads going through the same struggles, so I started sharing, and found the audience I have today.

/LAVENDAIRE
Aileen Xu
Subscribers: > 850k

Favourite YouTubers:
/AnnaAkana
/MarieForleo
/WillSmith

Dip the broccoli in chocolate

/WICKYDKEWL

Davey Wavey
Subscribers: > 1.1m

Favourite YouTubers:

/JonnaJinton
/TylerOakley
/MilesJaiProductions
/TestedCom
(Adam Savage's Tested)

Here's the thing. No one enjoys eating broccoli, because even though it's healthy and nutritious, it tastes like crap. In your videos, find the kernel of truth, the message, the wisdom being conveyed – the broccoli – but don't preach because it won't be interesting or accessible. Instead, package things up to make them more interesting, exciting, even titillating. That's the chocolate. I'm shirtless in a lot of my videos, and I say the skin pulls them in, but it's the message that keeps them watching. That's dipping the broccoli in chocolate.

Davey's story

I've been creating YouTube content for nearly 12 years. I started by using YouTube as an online diary, but my eighth video went viral. People – mostly gay men – started to subscribe, and I realized that there was an opportunity, even a responsibility, to engage with and support that community through video. I shifted my content, and instead of talking about books I was reading, I talked about things like coming out and self-acceptance. Now I make educational content for gay men. Our parents aren't gonna give us advice and we aren't going to learn it in school. YouTube is uniquely positioned so that each generation of gay men doesn't have to reinvent the gay wheel.

Make a channel trailer

/DIANAMADISON
Diana Madison
Subscribers: > 35k

Favourite YouTubers:
/HollyscoopTV
/CaptainWag (The Fumble)
/NerdWire
/DesireePerkinsMakeup

The channel trailer is really important: it must summarize your channel in less than three minutes. It means that whoever finds your channel will understand what you're about. Tell them you'll be uploading consistently, and give them a reason to stay and watch more, and to subscribe. Some of the most successful trailers are intense, well thought-out and empowering; they grab you and pull you in. That's the beauty of the trailer: you can give people the feeling that they are part of your world.

Diana's story

I wanted to host entertainment shows on TV, but it's hard to get into, so I decided to build my career on YouTube. Even my own parents thought I was crazy. As part of a contest for E! to be on the red carpet with Ryan Seacrest, I interviewed a friend who owns a clothing boutique, and uploaded the video to YouTube. I didn't win, but it got a lot of views. I realized I was on to something, so I started doing red-carpet interviews, getting access through my industry friends. I was one of the first, if not the first, YouTuber to do that, and now there are hundreds. Now the companies I used to work for compete with me and my channels to deliver the kind of numbers I'm getting.

Make that money, honey

Part of the allure of being YouTube famous is the money that goes with it. YouTubers rake in millions each year, but how do they do it? Here's how to get that green.

Partner up with YouTube

One of the easiest ways to make money is to participate in the YouTube Partner Program (YPP), in which YouTube sells ads that play before your videos and gives you a share of the profits. You can apply to YPP through the back-end of your YouTube channel, and you need to meet the following criteria to join:

- YPP is in your country

- You have more than 4,000 watch hours in the previous 12 months

- You have more than 1,000 subscribers

- You create content that meets the YPP policies

- You have an AdSense account.

Membership

YouTube has been rolling out a membership option where your fans can pay you a monthly membership fee. If you have access to this feature, your fans will see a Join button on your channel and video pages. When a fan becomes a member, they get things like special badges and access to perks that you've created just for them. The best part is that you'll receive 70 per cent of the revenue.

Donations and patronage

For a long time, Patreon has been the best way for YouTubers to allow their fans to contribute through a regular subscription. You can also use tools like GoFundMe, Indiegogo and Kickstarter if you are trying to secure funding for a specific project.

Brand partnerships and sponsorship

Make sure you put your email address on your About page, so that brands can contact you. Brands will pay YouTubers to review their products, wear their clothes or visit their hotels, or will simply sponsor them. For example, you'll see Ninja streaming himself playing *Fortnite* surrounded by merchandise from Red Bull, one of his sponsors.

Side hustle central

When you're really famous, you can sell merchandise – see Logan Paul's clothing range – or get paid for things like appearances at events and clubs. You could start a business, like Michelle Phan, who created Ipsy, a beauty company that is now valued at over $500 million.

Measure it

In YouTube Studio, the back-end tool you'll find in your YouTube channel, there's a whole section dedicated to analytics. Spending time here uncovers gems that will help you figure out what's working and what's not. There are tons of data and reports that you can use to make your channel and videos better, but here are a few of the most important I think you should look at regularly.

Watch time

Many people think video views are the most important metric on YouTube, but that's false. It's actually watch time. That's the total number of minutes that people have watched your videos. Simply put, videos and channels that have more watch time do better than those with less, so look at your analytics to see how much watch time your videos are accruing, and whether that number is going up or down. If some types of video you make garner more watch time than others, make more of those!

Traffic source

Traffic source will tell you how people found your videos. Maybe they came across you through 'Suggested Videos' or by searching YouTube, or perhaps they found you from external websites such as Facebook or a blog. You can often find clues as to how you can get more views by exploiting these sources. For example, if people are finding you through Reddit, perhaps you can post your videos there to increase your audience.

Subscribers

Subscribers are key to being a successful YouTuber, so check out your subscriber report to see how many people you have added each month, and how many people you've lost. The idea is to have a steadily growing stream of subscribers over time. If you're losing subscribers, stop and ask yourself why. Have you made a change to your videos recently that people don't like? Have you gained lots of subscribers thanks to a particular video? If so, try to replicate that success.

Illustrate to explain

/ASAPSCIENCE
Greg and Mitch
Subscribers: > 8.6m

Favourite YouTubers:
Greg: /KyleHanagami
Mitch: /ContraPoints

Both:
/Kurzgesagt (– In a Nutshell)

We've lasted on YouTube because our videos are visually animated, and because we aren't in the videos on our main channel. It's not that illustrated explainer videos are devoid of personality, but they are devoid of you, and that makes it easier to keep your audience. Sure, people will subscribe to a YouTuber just for their personality, but it can be hard to sustain personality-based fame. Illustrated explainer videos make complex subjects easy to understand with simple visuals and without big budgets, and can also be a great way to grow and keep your audience. Fans will fall in love with the content, reducing the risk that they'll fall out of love with you.

Greg and Mitch's story
We both studied biology at university, where we started dating. Greg minored in visual art and Mitch loved editing – he wasn't sure if he wanted a career in science or filmmaking. We enjoyed being the science guys explaining to friends what we had learned. Greg became a science teacher and realized that YouTube is a legitimate teaching tool, and Mitch started to work in editing with YouTubers, realizing that it's possible to make a living from this. We started a project together so that science wouldn't fall out of our lives. We made one video every week for a year. It was our third or fourth that went viral, which is unusually quick. Our aim is to make science accessible to as many people as possible.

Search out trends

/HALEYPHAM
Haley Pham
Subscribers: > 2.1m

Favourite YouTubers:
/KristinJohns
/ColleenVlogs
/rysphere (Ryan Trahan)

In order to grow your channel from nothing, you have to hop on the trends when they're relevant in order to be searched up and stumbled upon. Steal like an artist! Don't blatantly copy, but do keep it close enough to what is already working for other channels. Save being original for when you have an audience.

Haley's story

The summer before third grade, my dad showed me an app that would change my life forever: iMovie on his iPhone 3. That summer I began making short movies about my outfits or makeup and uploading them to my YouTube channel. It continued that way until my junior year in high school, when it became a viable career. Now it's the heart of all my business ventures and a full-time job that supports my mom and me.

Creative collaboration

JOB TITLE: DIRECTOR, CONTENT STRATEGY AT NBCUNIVERSAL MEDIA
COMPANY: NBCUNIVERSAL MEDIA

Working with an advertiser on branded content allows creators to bring to life passion projects. Think of it as a collaborative partnership vs. a random paycheque.

The marriage between a brand and a creator comes with a synergy that allows both parties to work together to innovate and creatively collaborate to push content boundaries, bringing something fresh and new to the platform – something that neither could have done on their own. When it's done right, the reaction from fans is incredible and they often feel pride and joy for that talent.

For example, Mamrie Hart writes amazing raps for her Audible shout-outs, when everyone else usually just reads the advertiser's talking points. Her fans can't get enough, and often comment 'They should double your paycheque!'

Getting educated

JOB TITLE: MANAGER OF CONTENT STRATEGY & PRODUCTION, SCALED EDUCATION
COMPANY: GOOGLE

Got questions? YouTube has answers
Have a burning question and can't seem to find the answer? Want to go deeper and improve your skills? Well, Matt Koval has everything you need to go from beginner to pro. Matt is a YouTuber and a YouTuber! He's been a creator with a popular comedy channel (www.youtube.com/user/MattKoval) and is a member of the YouTube team, where he creates content for YouTube's official educational resources for creators. I asked Matt where to go to get educated, get inspired and get answers. Here's what he recommends.

Subscribe to our two creator channels
Your first port of call should be our official channel for creator education and inspiration, the YouTube Creators Channel: www.youtube.com/user/CreatorAcademy. Here, YouTube experts and creators reveal their top tips. There's also an unofficial channel, Creator Insider, at www.youtube.com/CreatorInsider, which includes behind-the-scenes updates from the YouTube technical team.

Enrol in the Creator Academy
If you prefer to learn by way of guided online courses, consider the YouTube Creator Academy https://creatoracademy.youtube.com. We've got a huge catalogue of lessons and courses you can take to perfect your skills as a YouTuber, plus you can study with others and join a creator boot camp. It's all free.

Get help
If you have questions about the YouTube platform, its features and functions, our apps, tools and more, we have a Help Center, a searchable database of tech support answers: https://support.google.com/youtube. You can also subscribe to the TeamYouTube channel, www.youtube.com/user/YouTubeHelp, for tips and walkthroughs. These two resources should provide an answer to any question you might have.

Keep updated
We have two main blogs where we post announcements about things like new product features, and also letters from our CEO. We're at https://youtube.googleblog.com and https://youtube-creators.googleblog.com.

Visit a YouTube Space
Not many people know that we offer events, workshops and production resources to help bring your biggest ideas to life. You can visit a YouTube Space to produce video content, learn new skills and collaborate with the YouTube creative community. Creators with at least 10,000 subscribers and no strikes on their channel are able to apply. Apply at www.youtube.com/yt/space.

Let's connect
You can follow and interact with us on Twitter, at @YouTube, @TeamYouTube and @YTCreators. You can also find us on Instagram @YouTube. Add us!

Working with brands

JOB TITLE: SENIOR VICE PRESIDENT, NETWORK TALENT
COMPANY: STUDIO71

Do your research

I always counsel that if you're going to work with a brand, make sure it's one you agree with. For example, if you care about animal activism, only work with a makeup company that has a cruelty-free, no-animal-testing policy. If you don't do your research, your audience will, and they will call you out on it. The backlash has a ripple effect. I've unfortunately seen YouTubers (who weren't on my roster) make this kind of mistake, and then other brands wouldn't touch that creator because of the negativity associated with that brand deal. So, know the values of the people you are working with and ensure they align with yours.

Learn to be flexible

There is always a challenge when the creative you might normally make for your own channel isn't 100 per cent what the brand is looking for, so both sides need to be willing to compromise. Very few brands will just cut you a five-figure cheque so that you can do whatever you want without restriction. That's a unicorn, so learn to be flexible and work alongside the brand, otherwise they will feel as though you are working against them. That's why we refer to them as brand partnerships.

Keep it private

If things don't go well, don't talk about it publicly. If a brand integration goes wrong anywhere in the process, don't post about it, because it can come back to haunt you and could ruin future deals. If you talk a little trash on your Instagram or Twitter, it can follow you through the industry. It's important to remember that there are very few companies working in the space, so the person working at a network with you one day might be the person you work with at an agency in the future. You don't want to be known as the creator who is difficult to work with or the person who created social media drama.

Follow up

When things do go well, it's a missed opportunity not to follow up with a positive message of thanks. A lot of people don't take the time, and it's as simple as sending a note to the brand or agency. If you had a good time, tell them it was a pleasure working with them. I've even seen creators make mini recap videos to send to their client. That kind of thing is memorable, so go the extra mile to show you give a damn. In the same way that people talk when things go wrong, people talk when it goes right. You'll get more opportunities and deals by following up.

Disclose

It's so important to disclose in your videos when you're being paid by a brand. First off, it's legally required in the USA. But, arguably more importantly, be upfront and transparent about it with your fans, and that way your audience won't ever feel deceived. When you lose your audience's trust, it's gone forever.

Use your chips wisely

I often mention some advice from Dan Weinstein, the president and co-founder of Studio71 US, which is to use your chips wisely. Every creator has a finite number of chips, but it's different for everyone and you won't necessarily know how many you have. Let's say you're nominated for an award and you want your fans to vote for you. You can use some of your chips by asking them to vote, but you won't know how many chips it'll cost. The idea is this: don't ask more from your audience than is reasonable, but instead, use your chips wisely for what's important.

Above all else

Don't become a creator to become an influencer. Be a creator because you want to create.

Getting representation

JOB TITLE: PARTNER
COMPANY: SELECT MANAGEMENT GROUP

What does it mean to have representation?

Representation is effectively an agent or manager who works on your behalf to help you grow your profile, your business and your revenue. Their job is to regularly talk to brands and advertisers who have money to spend on a partnership with you, explaining the opportunity, showing them how it works and the value they'll get. For you, the YouTuber, your manager should stay on top of trends, new functionality and changes to the platform, and anything you might need to know to stay ahead. The idea is to make things easy for you so that you can focus on doing what you do best – making great content for your channel.

What makes for good representation?

Traditional talent agents and managers in the film and TV industry typically don't know a lot about the YouTube platform. YouTubers need someone who is on YouTube every day watching content, understanding what is and isn't working, which categories are surfacing and where there are business opportunities. Great managers typically have experience in the space, and have worked with other talent you'll recognize. For example, MyLifeAsEva came to us because she knew we worked with Gigi Gorgeous. You want to build a real relationship with your manager. You'll travel together, talk every day, celebrate the good times and weather the bad times. You'll develop a five-to-ten-year plan to grow your business. Plus, a good manager will let you vent; very few people can relate because they don't understand what YouTubers are doing.

If you're interested in working with brands or on special projects, you shouldn't be expected to read and understand a 25-page agreement, so having the support to handle it might make sense. It's a question of finding the balance that gives you the right resources to focus on your business while you work on making videos and interacting with your audience.

At what point should a YouTuber consider getting representation?

We get that question a lot. As you grow your channel, you'll grow your team. You might need an editor or a videographer first. Anyone you hire should take the weight off your shoulders so you can focus on making videos. There isn't an exact milestone, like a certain subscriber count, but if you see more incoming opportunities and you start to feel overwhelmed, that's a sign that you might need a manager. We don't proactively go out and sign people – people come to us through word-of-mouth referrals – but we do keep our eye on emerging talent, usually those with 250k subscribers and above. When we signed MyLifeAsEva she had 150k subscribers; she now has 9.5m on YouTube alone.

What makes a good client?

We want the combination of growth and engagement. A good client will work to grow their audience and engage with them. You should be able to sit in your bedroom and make a video, and then sit in the boardroom with an advertising executive. You need to be comfortable at a speaking appearance, being on social media and putting your life out there, being willing to share your livelihood with the world. You need to have a trajectory on the platform, meaning that you've hit on something that's working, and that you're growing as you produce content regularly. You need to feed the beast to succeed. We do also look for that IT factor; you have to have the personality.

So what do I do next?

Do your due diligence. See who is in the space and what's working for others, and ask your friends in the YouTube community to see who they are working with. You need to be sure before you build a new relationship with someone who will be taking a percentage from you. I will say 'No Uncles!' Don't have a family member be your manager. It's rarely a good idea. I suggest that YouTubers with smaller audiences sign up for a platform like Niche, Reelio or FameBit. You can decide later if you need a dedicated manager.

Growing your audience

JOB TITLE: PARTNER
COMPANY: LITTLE MONSTER MEDIA CO.

Post frequently

While this might be the least important of the three tactics, historically one of the best ways to increase your audience has been to upload more videos. YouTube has made some changes that help independent creators to be competitive even if they upload just once, twice or three times a week. It used to be that you had to post a new video every day, which for many is impossible. Try to post at least once a week, and more often if you can.

Boost your view duration

Your average view duration is the amount of time, on average, that people watch one of your videos. Based on our research, the real sweet spot across the board for your average view duration is 6–8 minutes. Sure, there are plenty of successful channels that don't get that much duration, but if you can generate that amount of time spent, it'll help a lot.

Increase your click-through rate

Probably the most important factor for increasing your audience is improving your click-through rate (CTR) – that is, the number of times your video was shown and then clicked on. YouTube tells you how many impressions your title and thumbnail get, along with your CTR. This has been a real game-changer. The stronger your title and thumbnail, the better your CTR. Remember, though, that you should stick to making videos that work within your programming choice. What I mean by that is that if you make videos that are listicles about superheroes, don't suddenly start making an explainer video about how to bake chocolate-chip cookies. Your CTR is closely based on what your core audience wants to see from you, so making something unexpected will get a low CTR – even if your baking video is great.

Bonus tip

Metadata, things like adding tags to your videos, don't appear to do much these days, so only spend a few minutes on this. Instead, spend an hour perfecting your thumbnail.

Multi-Channel Networks (MCNs)

JOB TITLE: MANAGING DIRECTOR
COMPANY: KIN

What is an MCN?

Multi-Channel Networks are always evolving, but they started by selling advertising media across a collection of YouTube channels they'd represent, connecting YouTubers with brands that wanted influencer marketing campaigns, and by providing support services to those YouTubers. Now MCNs can offer more, things like representation, technical expertise, analytics help, licensing help, creating merchandise and audience growth strategies. Many are a hybrid of an agent, a production company, a media company, a management team and even an e-commerce platform.

What's Kin?

Kin was one of the earliest MCNs, but as the space got crowded, we evolved into a broader lifestyle entertainment company. We work with creators, we have production capabilities and relationships with brands and their creative and media agencies, and we develop strategies, campaigns and original content across many media platforms.

Should I work with an MCN?

Sure, but with so many facets to MCNs, it comes back to 'What do you need?' That dictates who you should work with. Start by doing your homework and researching MCNs. Not all are created equal, and they all offer different things. Before you even talk to them, ask yourself where you need help. Most YouTubers are looking for help connecting with brands who want to pay them to create content.

Ask the MCN:

'What value are you providing to my business?'

'What ongoing support will I have and what will that support look like?'

'Who will be my main point of contact and how reachable are they?'

Be sure that the revenue you are giving to your MCN is equivalent to the value you're getting from them.

Pro tip

Really lean in on the clauses around terminating the partnership. That's where I see a lot of people running into trouble: they aren't clear on termination periods and find themselves locked into contracts longer than they should be. The idea of consulting a lawyer when you are a small concern might feel a bit over the top, but I would recommend it. It's a contract, and you need to treat it with a certain level of seriousness.

Pro tip

If you're going to talk to an MCN, be prepared to speak quickly about your audience statistics. You should know your key demographics and how your audience breaks down globally. Be forthcoming with your data and analytics; don't keep anything behind the curtain. This can be as simple as providing a screenshot of your analytics and your last 90 days' performance.

Index

ABOUT THE AUTHOR

Will Eagle is a seasoned brand, marketing and digital professional, having worked at Virgin, MTV, Leo Burnett, Google and YouTube. At Google, Will was a brand strategist focused on helping the company's biggest advertising clients understand how they could use YouTube to meet their marketing needs. Will was Google's Chief Facilitator at the PartnerPlex in Mountain View, and an advisor to the portfolio companies of Capital G, Google's late-stage venture-capital fund.

Born in the UK, Will started his career as a web developer for the Virgin Group in London, before moving to Canada in 2004, and then to the USA in 2014. He spends as much time as possible in his cabin in rural Ontario, and loves creative approaches to problem-solving at scale, slow-cookers, spending time in nature and playing *Fortnite*.

ACKNOWLEDGEMENTS

With my love and thanks to every YouTuber I had the opportunity to learn from, and with deepest gratitude to Andrew Hayes, Neha Sharma, Francisco Chacin, Matt Sweet, Marissa Orr, Jay V. del Rosario, Sam Sutherland, Ashley Carter, Reuven Ashtar, Mark Swierszcz, Jordan Bortolotti, Rick Matthews, Matt Kovalakides, Adam Goldstein, Renata Duque, John Carle, Adam Wescott and Charley Button.

Very special thanks to Henry Carroll, Heshan Withana, Jo Lightfoot, Melissa Danny, Sandra Assersohn, Andrew Roff, Alex Coco, Rosie Fairhead, Robert Davies, Christine Shuttleworth and the whole team at Laurence King.

READ THIS
IF YOU WANT
TO BE GREAT
AT DRAWING.
SELWYN LEAMY

READ THIS
IF YOU WANT
TO TAKE GREAT
PHOTOGRAPHS.
HENRY CARROLL

READ
THIS.

USE THIS
IF YOU WANT
TO TAKE GREAT
PHOTOGRAPHS.
A photo journal
HENRY CARROLL

READ THIS
IF YOU WANT TO BE
INSTAGRAM FAMOUS.

Be inspired by
the other books
in this bestselling
series from
Laurence King.

LAURENCE KING

READ THIS
IF YOU WANT
TO TAKE GREAT
PHOTOGRAPHS
OF PEOPLE.
HENRY CARROLL

READ THIS
IF YOU WANT
TO TAKE GREAT
PHOTOGRAPHS
OF PLACES.
HENRY CARROLL

Read This
if You Want to Take
Great Photographs

This bestselling, jargon-free book walks you through the fundamentals of photography and introduces you to the work of some must-know masters.

978 1 78067 335 6

Read This
if You Want to Be
Instagram Famous

Featuring tips from 50 of the hottest Instagrammers around, this book holds the secrets to fixing up your feed and finding thousands of followers.

978 1 78067 967 9

Read This
if You Want to Take
Great Photographs of People

Ideal for users of any camera, this book contains the essential techniques of photographing people, whether that's on the street, at home or in the studio.

978 1 78067 624 1

Read This
if You Want to Be
Great at Drawing

Featuring essential techniques used by artists past and present, this book will sharpen up your drawing skills across a variety of media.

978 1 78627 054 2

Read This
if You Want to Take
Great Photographs of Places

Packed with practical tips and iconic images, this accessible book arms you with the know-how you need to take meaningful pictures of the places that matter to you most.

978 1 78067 905 1

Read This
if You Want to Be
Great At Drawing People

This accessible and jargon-free guide to drawing faces and figures features examples of great drawings by masters and contemporary artists.

978 1 7862 7512 7

Use This
if You Want to Take
Great Photographs

With fun photography prompts and inspiring images by acclaimed photographers, this journal is just what you need to get creative with your camera.

978 1 78067 888 7

Use This
if You Want To Be
Great At Drawing

A playful introduction to contemporary drawing style, techniques and ideas with fun and inspiring prompts to help unlock your imagination.

978 1 7862 7405 2